JOHN P. WEBSTER
LIBRARY
Resources for Faith & Life

Ruth Dudley Collection

at
First Church, West Hartford
12 South Main Street
West Hartford, CT 06107

www.whfirstchurch.org/jp-webster-library
860-232-3893

Parable of the Bridesmaids

WRITTEN AND ILLUSTRATED BY
Helen Caswell

Abingdon Press
Nashville

PARABLE OF THE BRIDESMAIDS

Library of Congress Cataloging-in-Publication Data

CASWELL, HELEN RAYBURN.
 Parable of the bridesmaids/written and illustrated by Helen Caswell.
  p. cm.
 Summary: Retells Jesus' parable of the ten bridesmaids, five of whom prepared for their part in the wedding festivities and five of whom were foolish.
 ISBN 0-687-30022-3 (alk. paper)
 1. Ten virgins (Parable)—Juvenile literature. 2. Bible stories, English—N. T. Matthew. [Ten virgins (Parable)
 2. Parables. 3. Bible stories—N.T.] I. Title.
 BT378.T4C377 1992
 226.8'09505—dc20   91-36857
                                                                  AC

Printed in Hong Kong

Read Matthew 25:1-13

There was going to be a wedding!
Ten girls had been asked to be bridesmaids. They were all excited, because a wedding was more fun than anything they could imagine.

The wedding would be at night.
First, the bridegroom would go to the home of the
bride. Then there would be a procession to the
place where there would be a wonderful party and feast.

The bridesmaids were supposed to meet the bridegroom when he arrived, and then be in the
procession with their lamps.

Now, five of these bridesmaids were very sensible girls. They carefully got ready for the wedding, and made sure that they had enough oil for their lamps.

The other five bridesmaids were silly. They went to the wedding without even thinking to see if there was enough oil for their lamps.

Finally, they got to the town where the wedding was to be. The bridegroom had not yet arrived, and the bridesmaids settled down to wait for him. They were so tired from their long walk that they went to sleep.

At midnight there was shouting in the street — "The bridegroom is here! Bring the lamps!"

They had gone only a little way when five of the lamps sputtered out.

The five silly bridesmaids cried out to the other five, "Our lamps are out of oil! Give us some of yours!"

But the sensible bridesmaids said, "No, then *we* might run out! You'll just have to buy your own oil!"

Of course, it was so late that all the shops were closed. The five silly bridesmaids ran to the shop that sold oil, and banged on the door and cried until the man finally opened his shop and sold them some oil. But it took a long time.

The silly bridesmaids
filled their lamps, lit
them, and rushed back
to the wedding. But the
procession was all over.
They were too late!
The door to the bride-
groom's house was
closed and locked.
Everyone was inside,
having such a fine,
noisy time at the party
that they couldn't hear
the silly bridesmaids
weeping and banging
on the door.

Jesus said that this story is like the kingdom of God. We must always be prepared for anything God wants us to do.

BJO

RUTH DUDLEY RESOURCE CENTER
125 SHERMAN STREET
HARTFORD, CONNECTICUT 06105